Clara
Barton

An 1875 photograph of Clara Barton wearing a brooch decorated with the symbol of the Red Cross

JUNIOR ■ WORLD ■ BIOGRAPHIES

Clara Barton

LIZ SONNEBORN

CHELSEA JUNIORS

a division of CHELSEA HOUSE PUBLISHERS

Chelsea House Publishers
EDITOR-IN-CHIEF: Remmel Nunn
MANAGING EDITOR: Karyn Gullen Browne
COPY CHIEF: Juliann Barbato
PICTURE EDITOR: Adrian G. Allen
ART DIRECTOR: Maria Epes
DEPUTY COPY CHIEF: Mark Rifkin
ASSISTANT ART DIRECTOR: Noreen Romano
MANUFACTURING MANAGER: Gerald Levine
SYSTEMS MANAGER: Lindsey Ottman
PRODUCTION MANAGER: Joseph Romano
PRODUCTION COORDINATOR: Marie Claire Cebrián

JUNIOR WORLD BIOGRAPHIES

EDITOR: Remmel Nunn

Staff for CLARA BARTON
PICTURE RESEARCHERS: Cheryl Moch, Diane Wallis, Jonathan Shapiro
SENIOR DESIGNER: Marjorie Zaum
COVER ILLUSTRATION: Michael Garland

3 5 7 9 8 6 4

Library of Congress Cataloging-in-Publication Data
Sonneborn, Liz.
    Clara Barton/Liz Sonneborn.
        p. cm.—(Junior world biographies)
    Summary: Presents the life of the nurse who served on the battlefields of the
Civil War and later founded the American Red Cross.
    ISBN 0-7910-1565-3
    1. Barton, Clara, 1821–1912—Juvenile literature. 2. Nurses—United
States—Biography—Juvenile literature. 3. Red Cross—United States—
Biography—Juvenile literature. [1. Barton, Clara, 1821–1912. 2. Nurses.
3. American National Red Cross.] I. Title. II. Series.
HV569.B3S66 1992
361.7'634'092—dc20   90-21398
[B]   CIP
[92]   AC

Contents

Timid by nature, young Clara quickly developed confidence whenever she was called upon to help others.

1

A Shy
Little Girl

Just before sunset on Christmas Day in 1871, Clara Barton was startled by a knock on her door. She was living in Strasbourg, a French city that had been devastated by war. Thousands of people had been killed, and hundreds of buildings had been destroyed. With other volunteers, Barton was helping the survivors rebuild their lives.

When Barton opened the door, she spied a crowd of people gathered around the tallest

Christmas tree she had ever seen. On every branch was a lighted candle, glittering brightly against the darkening sky. The inhabitants of Strasbourg had brought the tree to Barton as a token of thanks for everything she had done for them. Fittingly, their gift was presented on a special day for Barton, her birthday. Far from home in a war-torn city, she was delighted to have so many friends to help her celebrate.

Fifty years earlier and thousands of miles away, the Barton household in Massachusetts was the setting of another birthday celebration. The four Barton children—Dorothy, Stephen, David, and Sally—whooped and cheered when they learned of the birth of their baby sister. Their parents named the infant Clarissa, after a character in a popular novel. But from the start her brothers and sisters rarely called her that, preferring to use the pet names Tot or Baby instead. Eventually, though, they all settled on Clara as the nickname that best suited the youngest Barton.

As a girl, Clara lived in the small town of North Oxford. The rocky terrain in North Oxford made the land difficult to farm, but the lush forests covering the hillsides made lumbering a profitable business. Clara's ancestors had been prominent farmers and lumber-mill owners in the town for more than 100 years.

Sitting by the fire on long winter evenings, young Clara heard her father's tales of how the Bartons came to this beautiful country. Captain Stephen Barton told her that they were among the first English families to sail to North America in the 17th century. Many of these early Barton settlers and their children became important politicians and soldiers in Massachusetts Bay Colony long before the United States was a country.

Clara enjoyed these stories, but she loved Captain Barton's tales of his own military adventures even more. Before he married Clara's mother, he had traveled to what is now Michigan to fight with American forces against the Indians living there. In his three years with these troops,

Clara's father, Stephen, loved to tell her stories about his days as a soldier.

Clara's father suffered extreme hardships, but he made his experiences into dramatic stories that his youngest daughter begged to hear again and again. In one tale, he was wounded and separated from his fellow soldiers. Left without food or water for days, he was near death when he spotted a set of paw prints that a wild dog had left in the mud. He drank the rainwater that had collected in the tracks and then followed them to find the unfortunate animal, which became the soldier's dinner.

Through his stories, the captain taught Clara not only about the life of a soldier but also about the importance of self-discipline and self-control. Her mother, Sarah, instilled the same values in her daughter, but in different ways. Practical and firm, Sarah Barton was an extremely hard worker who, Clara later wrote, "always did two days' work in one." She demanded the same diligence from Clara. Forbidden from wasting her time with toys, Clara even as a little girl was expected to help her mother with all the household chores.

In addition to her mother's and father's lessons, Clara learned a great many things from her brothers and sisters, who were much older than Clara. The closest in age was Sally, who was 11 years old when Clara was born. As an adult, Clara remembered that she felt as though she had "six fathers and mothers" who "all took charge of me, all educated me according to personal taste." From Dorothy, Stephen, and Sally—all of whom would grow up to become schoolteachers—Clara learned about poetry, mathematics, and geography. Although an eager pupil for these bookish subjects, Clara liked David's lessons best. When she was only three, her gentle brother taught her how to ride a horse. She loved the freedom she felt on horseback and always thought of David as a hero for introducing her to it.

Although she had many teachers, young Clara had few playmates. Growing up around no children her own age, she felt lonely much of the time. Clara was also timid, sometimes so much so that common things such as thunderstorms and snakes filled her with terror.

Hoping to help Clara overcome her shyness, her parents sent her to boarding school when she was nine. But away from her family, her fears grew even worse. Scared of strangers, she was unable to talk to the other students. Her teachers became concerned, especially after the nervous girl stopped eating. Although they thought Clara was a fine student, in the end they decided it was best to send her home.

Clara was born in this house in North Oxford, Massachusetts.

Back in North Oxford, Clara's embarrassing memories of her failure at school quickly faded when David was injured in a fall. Soon after, he developed a fever, and his doctors prescribed a common cure of the time—bloodletting. This treatment involved placing bloodsucking worms called leeches on the patient's body. The leeches would suck up the "bad blood" that the doctors believed was causing the illness. Clara, who refused to leave David's side, overcame her fear of leeches and learned to place and remove the worms without hurting her ailing brother.

After weeks of this therapy, David showed no signs of improvement. The doctors and his parents gave up hope. Only Clara still believed that David could recover. She stayed by his side day and night for two years, doing everything she could think of to make him comfortable and help him get well. As time went by, she became an able nurse, always quick to guess her brother's needs. Her family found it hard to believe that this confident, competent young girl was the same Clara who only years before was too bashful to speak to children she did not know.

David finally began to get better after his parents consulted a new doctor. This physician told the Bartons to stop the bloodletting and give the boy steam baths instead. The new treatment probably did not help David, but ending the old therapy did. As doctors know today, bloodletting can cause a patient more harm than good. David most likely would have recovered much faster had the leechings never been prescribed. But certainly he would never have survived at all without Clara's dedicated care.

Clara was thrilled that David was well at last. Yet secretly she missed having a patient to nurse. Clara began to look for other activities that could make her feel as useful as caring for her brother had.

For a time, Clara helped her now grown sister Sally care for her children. But this role as helper was not enough for Clara. Despite her mother's objections, she took a job weaving cotton cloth at a mill her brother Steven had opened several years earlier. She loved the work, but the mill burned down two weeks later, leaving her again without an occupation. She then began to devote most of her time to helping her poorer neighbors.

Clara's charity was especially needed during an epidemic of smallpox, a then deadly disease that swept through North Oxford when she was in her early teens. Often with little sleep for days

A no-nonsense woman, Sarah Stone Barton taught her youngest daughter the value of hard work and discipline.

at a time, the young nurse held the hands of the sick, wiped their foreheads with damp cloths, and prepared their meals.

Clara's neighbors were very grateful for her nursing. But despite their appreciation and attention, Clara still became bashful and fearful whenever she had no patients to care for. Her behavior worried her family and especially perplexed her mother. A no-nonsense woman, Sarah Barton became angry when Clara wept at the slightest criticism or hid when something was bothering her rather than tell her family what was wrong. Clara's stern mother had no idea what to do about her difficult daughter.

Clara herself shared some of Sarah Barton's confusion. Every day, Clara wished for something to happen that would give her life direction. At last, when she was 15 years old, a visit from an unusual stranger with some unexpected advice did just that.

Barton sat for this photograph while she was a student at the Clinton Liberal Institute, a college in New York State.

CHAPTER

2
School Days

Barton woke suddenly and, for a moment, could not remember where she was. In a sleepy haze, she looked around and slowly recognized the sitting room of her home. Sick with the mumps, Barton had accidentally fallen asleep on the couch.

As she sat up, she heard voices in the next room. One was her mother's. The other belonged to a man she did not know. Barton then heard her mother say her name. Curious, Barton crept

19

to the doorway so she could better understand what they were saying. Sarah Barton was asking what she could do to help her youngest daughter overcome her shyness. For the rest of her life, Barton remembered the man's response: "The sensitive nature will always remain. She will never assert herself for herself; she will suffer wrong first, but for others she will be perfectly fearless. Throw responsibility upon her." He then suggested that Barton study to become a teacher.

The Bartons' guest was Lorenzo Niles Fowler, an Englishman who had come to North Oxford to deliver a lecture. Fowler was a believer in phrenology, a study that held that people's characters and special talents were caused by the shape of the brain and skull. During his lectures, Fowler maintained that by feeling a person's head to find bumps and bulges on the skull he could discover the person's true calling in life.

Scientists have since disproved the beliefs of phrenologists. Nevertheless, Fowler's advice for Barton was sound. Both Barton and her family agreed that she would make a fine teacher. Barton studied hard for one more year, and at 17 she was hired to teach at a one-room schoolhouse on the other side of town.

Even though she was excited about her new job, Barton's old fears began to get the better of her as the first day of school approached. She was to teach 40 pupils, including 4 boys her own age. They were well known for making trouble. Barton had even heard a rumor that their old teacher had quit after the boys locked her out of the schoolhouse. If Barton were to do her job well, she would have to find a way to command the boys' respect.

Finally, the big day came. Barton arrived at the school wearing a new green dress with a long skirt that she hoped would make her look older. She also had her hair piled up high on her head to make her look taller than her mere five feet. But, despite these preparations, when she was standing in front of her class looking into her students' faces, she panicked.

Not knowing what to say, she reached for a Bible on her desk. She opened it and began to read aloud. Her courage came back as she realized that the room was silent except for the sound of her strong, clear voice. Even the four oldest boys were listening.

Barton won another victory in the school yard that day. The four older boys were playing ball and asked Barton to join the game. To their surprise, she was an excellent player, better than any of them. The troublemakers then forgot any pranks they had planned to play on the new teacher.

By the end of the term, Barton had proved herself to school officials in North Oxford as well. They gave her an award for having the best-disciplined class in the entire district. Barton was slightly embarrassed by the honor. She explained that she had never had to discipline any of her students because they never misbehaved.

For the next 10 years, Barton taught in many schools in North Oxford and nearby villages. Her confidence grew. So did her reputation as a teacher. Officials and parents respected her, and her pupils loved her. Many of them as adults wrote to Barton to thank her, sometimes crediting

As a young woman, Barton became interested in phrenology. Phrenologists believed that the shapes of people's skulls reveal their special talents.

her teaching for the successes they had had in life. Barton returned their affection. As an old woman, she wrote that "they were all mine" and that her love for her pupils was second only to that of their own mothers.

Barton was never to have a husband and children of her own, but as a young woman she had many suitors. One named Oliver Williams begged Barton to marry him. He was so hurt when she refused that he left North Oxford, traveling to California where gold had been discovered. After he made a fortune in the West, Williams returned to Massachusetts. He hoped his money would impress Barton enough to make her change her mind, but she gently told him no once again. According to a close friend, Barton did not marry Williams because she did not think he was very interesting. Years later, the friend speculated that Barton was never tempted to wed because she "was herself so much stronger a character than any of the men who [courted] her."

Barton's social life was busy during her

first years as a teacher, but most of her time was devoted to improving the schools in North Oxford. One of her many projects was establishing a school for the poor children of workers at the local mills. Winning the townspeople's support, Barton was told she could use a room in the largest mill for her school.

There, Barton faced her greatest challenge as a teacher. She had 70 students, ranging in age from 4 to 24. Most of the students had been born in Europe and knew little English. Adding to Barton's problems was the classroom itself. It was so dark that she had to leave the outer door open in order to let in enough light for her students to read. Unfortunately, the open door also let in the noise from the street. Occasionally, a stray goat from a nearby farm wandered inside.

But Barton now had the confidence to overcome these obstacles. She quickly taught the poor students to read and do basic arithmetic and then moved on to more difficult subjects such as philosophy, chemistry, and ancient history. The community hailed the mill school as a great success.

Barton loved teaching. But, in 1850, she decided she was ready for a new adventure. After a 200-mile train ride, she arrived in Clinton, New York, where she enrolled in the Clinton Liberal Institute. At that time, the school at Clinton was one of the few academies for female teachers in the entire United States.

Barton enjoyed her classes and sometimes studied by lamplight well into the night. She made many new friends as well. But what she liked best at Clinton was living away from home. Now, she finally felt that she was on her own.

But two problems soon disrupted her new found freedom. One involved money. Over the years, Barton had saved much of her teaching income, but teachers, most of whom were women, were paid very little. At Clinton, she found that her tuition and expenses quickly amounted to more than her savings. Sadly, she realized she could not afford to stay in school. At about the same time, she received terrible news from Stephen. Their mother had died suddenly. The mail in those days traveled so slowly that the funeral had already taken place by the time Stephen's letter reached Barton. Nevertheless, she got on a train and returned home to mourn with her family.

Barton's life had been so busy that after a few idle weeks in North Oxford she became restless. When a classmate from Clinton invited Barton to visit her house in Heightstown, New Jersey, Barton eagerly accepted. While there, she was persuaded to take a teaching job in nearby Bordentown.

Barton liked the town but not her new school, mostly because the students had to pay to attend it. Barton believed education should be free. Her objections to the school's policy grew when she discovered that it was the only one in town. There was no school at all for the town's poor children.

For months, she led a campaign to create a free school. The town school board did not like the idea at first. Some members said that the poor

Teaching in this schoolhouse in Bordentown, New Jersey, Barton earned the love and respect of her many students.

did not need or deserve an education. But when Barton would not give up, they told her she could use a shabby, vacant building as a schoolhouse.

On the first day of school, Barton arrived to find the building empty. The poor children of Bordentown had never been to school. Not knowing what to expect, they had been too scared to show up.

Barton walked outside, dreading the school board's jeers when they discovered her free school was a failure. In the school yard, she was surprised to see six boys nervously hanging around. She said hello and asked them a few questions about themselves, gradually gaining their confidence. They soon followed her inside. Seeing the maps on the schoolhouse walls, they asked her about foreign countries they wanted to visit. She told them fascinating stories she had read about these places.

That evening, the boys told their friends about the odd, small woman who knew so much. The next day, there were 20 students in Barton's class. By the end of the week, the number had doubled. Two years later, the school board financed the building of a new two-story schoolhouse with eight classrooms. Its enrollment swelled to 600.

The townspeople were proud of the new free school and of Barton. But when it came time to select a teacher to head the school, the board hired a man named J. Kirby Burham. The board members told Barton that the job was too important for a woman to hold. She was to be Burham's assistant and receive a salary worth only half of his.

Barton was outraged. After all, she had started the school and made it a success. She continued to teach at Bordentown for a while. But, angry and exhausted, she became ill. One day, she rose before her class and discovered she had lost her voice. Unable to speak, she resigned her post.

Although Barton did not tell Stephen all of her troubles, he sensed her unhappiness in her letters. He begged her to come back to North Oxford. But in 1854, much to his surprise, he received word that she had moved to Washington, D.C. Instead of going home, Barton had decided to start a new life in a new city.

The famous photographer Mathew Brady took this picture of Barton during the Civil War years.

CHAPTER

3

Angel of
the Battlefield

Barton told her friends that she decided to move to Washington, D.C., because the mild climate would help her recover her health. But she was probably also attracted by the excitement of the nation's capital. Much of her first weeks in Washington were spent in the Library of Congress. She slowly regained her voice but began to complain of eyestrain due to reading in its dim lighting. Barton also enjoyed visiting the sessions of Congress. There, she learned firsthand about the workings of the U.S. government by listening to congressmen debate the issues of the day.

Slowly, Barton made friends in Washington. Among them was Alexander DeWitt, a congressman from Massachusetts. When Barton told DeWitt that she needed to find work, he introduced her to Charles Mason, who headed the U.S. Patent Office. Like DeWitt, Mason was struck by Barton's intelligence and offered her a job as a clerk.

Barton took the job, becoming one of only a handful of women who then held government posts. She liked the work and was especially pleased by her salary. Unlike teaching school, this job paid well.

As always, Barton proved herself to be a hard worker. Even so, many of her fellow clerks disliked her. They did not think it was proper for a woman to work in an office alongside men. They also felt that she should be paid less, not because she did less work, but just because she was female. Some of the clerks made unkind comments about

Barton and blew cigarette smoke in her face. One even spat tobacco juice at her. Throughout the ordeal, Mason stuck by Barton. But in August 1857, he resigned his post. Without his support, she lost her job.

Barton packed up her things and returned to North Oxford. Her plan was to have a brief visit with her family while she looked for work. But years passed, and she still had not found another clerkship. Despite her experience and talent, no one wanted to hire a woman for what was considered "man's work." Just as Barton had given up hope, the U.S. Patent Office offered her a temporary job in late 1860. It paid less than her old one had, but, desperately needing money, she accepted it.

Barton found that Washington had changed in the time she had been away. Abraham Lincoln had just been elected president, and the government was in turmoil. For many years, the states in the North had been bickering with the states in the South. The two sides disagreed on many issues, but the one that caused the most tension was slavery. In the South, black slaves were forced to work on large farms, called plantations, owned by rich white men. In the North, where most people's income came from industry rather than from farming, slavery was against the law. Many Northerners wanted to end, or abolish, slavery in the South as well. But most Southerners thought the abolitionists had no right to tell them what to do. To them, the election of Lincoln, who wanted to forbid slavery in any new states, was the last straw.

Just before Barton arrived in Washington, South Carolina declared that it no longer wanted to be part of the United States. Other Southern states planned to follow its lead. Northern leaders wanted the North and the South to remain united, but it was growing clear that it would take a war to hold the country together. On April 14, 1861, the first shots were fired when Southerners attacked Northern forces at Fort Sumter near Charleston, South Carolina. The Civil War had begun.

Lincoln immediately summoned thousands of volunteer troops to Washington. Suddenly, the streets of the capital were flooded with soldiers. The scene filled Barton with frustration. She wished that she too could fight to save the nation. "I'm well and strong and young—young enough to go to the front," Barton told a friend. But she knew a woman would never be allowed to join the battle. "If I can't be a soldier," she vowed, "I'll help soldiers."

Her chance soon came. Among the volunteers that arrived in Washington was a regiment from Massachusetts. Barton rushed to the train station, hoping to spot some of her old friends and students. She was shocked by what she saw there. Even though the regiment had yet to spend a day on the battlefield, all of the men were bloody and ragged. Dozens were wounded. On the way to Washington, they had been attacked by crowds of angry Southerners.

The army was not prepared to help men in their condition. It barely had enough food for the new recruits, let alone any clothing or medicine. If the soldiers were to receive help, Barton realized, it would have to come from her. She sped home and packed up all the food, soap, and candles she had on hand. She then tore up her sheets to make towels and bandages and, using her own money, bought some clothing for the men. It took five men to carry the boxes of goods to the regiment.

Barton knew the supplies would not last long. She sat down and wrote letter after letter to

Women were not allowed to be soldiers. However, many aided troops by feeding, clothing, and caring for the wounded.

the soldiers' mothers, telling them what had happened. Soon boxes arrived from Massachusetts, filled with everything the men needed. So many came that Barton had to rent three warehouses to store them all.

The smiles and kind words of the soldiers made Barton feel she was making a real contribution to the war effort. Yet, as the fighting increased, she began to think it was not enough. The stories of men who had been to the front haunted her. They said that there were so few doctors that hours or even days passed before the wounded received treatment. Infections sometimes killed soldiers with minor wounds. Some wounded men even died of thirst because there was no one to fetch them water.

Barton thought back on how well she had nursed her brother David when they were children. She knew she could help these men. But no proper woman would go to a battlefield, and besides, the army would never let her. Yet, as Barton later wrote, she could not stop hearing "the groans of suffering men dying like dogs." If going to the front would silence them, then she had no choice but to do it.

Barton found it was difficult to persuade government officials to agree to her plan. Most claimed that the army had all the supplies and medical help it needed. But they had not been to battle, and all the soldiers who had been disagreed. Barton kept up her campaign. In 1862, the surgeon general of the United States finally relented and issued her a military pass.

The first battlefield Barton saw was at Cedar Mountain in Virginia. Traveling alone in a wagon packed with supplies, she arrived just as army surgeon James I. Dunn had run out of bandages. In a letter to his wife, Dunn wrote that when he saw Barton and her wagon, he felt that heaven had sent him an angel. During the war, the letter was published in many Northern newspapers. Barton became famous as the Angel of the Battlefield.

Several weeks later, Barton received word that a battle had begun in Bull Run field near

Thousands of men from both the North and the South were killed in brutal Civil War battles.

Fairfax, Virginia. Eight thousand men had already been killed, and the fighting was still raging. She boarded a train headed for the battlefield, riding in a boxcar loaded with supplies. As the train drew into Fairfax Station, Barton looked out of the boxcar door onto an incredible scene. Acres of wooded hillside were covered with wounded men lying on a bedding of hay. Jumping from the train, Barton hiked up her skirt, pinned it to her waist, and got to work.

Wagons filled with soldiers kept coming. By the end of the day, 3,000 bodies blanketed the slope. Barton and the three female volunteers she had brought with her fed and washed the wounds of as many soldiers as they could. Some men, almost dead from hunger, wept when the women handed them meager portions of soup and bread. The nurses labored long into the night. Working by candlelight, they had to move carefully as they stepped between the bodies. If a candle dropped onto the hay, the entire hillside, including the helpless men, would go up in flames.

The war continued, and Barton traveled

from battle to battle with little chance for rest in between. At each battlefield, she witnessed new horrors. At Chantilly, Virginia, for instance, she recognized the gunpowder-stained face of a recruit as that of one of the four troublemakers she had so impressed on her first day as a teacher. The reunion was a sad experience for Barton. As they reminisced, she had to bandage the young man's mangled arm.

Barton labored on the Chantilly battlefield for five days and nights, most of the time in the pouring rain. When she was so exhausted she could barely stand, a messenger came to her with word that the North had lost the battle. Their forces were retreating, closely followed by Southern troops. If she did not leave immediately, she was sure to be captured by the enemy. Within minutes, Barton was on a train. But before she stepped aboard, she made sure all of the wounded were on the train as well. As the engine moved out of the station, Barton watched as the Southern forces rode into view.

This was not Barton's only narrow escape.

Barton treated many wounded soldiers, such as these waiting for aid after the Battle of Fredericksburg.

At the Battle of Antietam, a wounded man lying on the ground asked her for some water. Kneeling down, she held out a cup and slowly raised his head toward it. Suddenly, a shot rang out. The bullet burst through the sleeve of her dress and into the poor soldier's chest. The man fell back dead.

Another soldier at Antietam begged Barton for her help. He had been shot in the face, and a musket ball was wedged in his cheek. The pain was excruciating. When the man asked Barton to remove the ball, she explained that she was a nurse, not a surgeon. She said she would hurt him if she tried. This made the soldier smile, as best he could. They both realized that a surgeon would not be free to tend him for hours. He assured Barton that no pain she could cause would be worse than what he would feel while waiting. Asking a sergeant to hold her patient's head still, Barton bravely grabbed a pocketknife, cut open the soldier's face, and pulled the musket ball free.

Barton's courage at the front never left her. Just as in the past, as long as she was helping others she could ignore thoughts of her own well-being. But before this her fears had usually been groundless. The snakes and thunderstorms that scared her as a child posed no real threat. Her terror of failing as an adult had been foolish in light of her skills and intelligence. As a battlefield nurse, though, every day could easily have been her last. She was well aware of the danger she was in. But she also knew how many lives she was saving. In the face of that, the danger seemed to matter very little.

Tales of Barton's courage and charity made her famous in both the United States and Europe.

CHAPTER

4

European
Adventures

On April 9, 1865, the South admitted defeat
and surrendered to Northern forces. The Civil
War had finally ended. But the tragic conse-
quences of the fighting were far from over. Vast
amounts of land and property had been destroyed. Even worse was the number of casualties.
Hundreds of thousands of men had been killed.

Barton had seen the suffering of many
men. But one man's pain had touched her especially deeply. At the beginning of the war, her

brother Stephen had been in North Carolina, a Southern state. For years, the Barton family had tried to find out if he was safe, but no word could get through the battle lines. One day, out of the blue, Barton received a letter from Stephen. He had been taken prisoner by the Northern army and was very sick. Barton immediately begged her friends in the army for help. They saw to it that Stephen was freed and sent to Barton. She nursed him for many months. But even her skilled help could not save him. Only one month before the surrender, Stephen died.

After the war, Barton received hundreds of letters from families of missing men. The writers had read stories of her bravery on the battlefield, which had been published in many newspapers. They wrote Barton on the slim chance that she would remember nursing their loved ones.

Still mourning Stephen, Barton's heart went out to the families of the missing. She wished there was something she could do, but there was no organization for finding missing soldiers that she could join. While answering a particularly moving letter, an idea finally struck her. If no such organization existed, then she would form one herself.

Barton started compiling lists of names of the missing, which she persuaded newspapers across the country to print. If anyone knew the whereabouts of a man on one of the lists, the person could write to Barton. She would then pass the information along to the writer's family. Barton was thrilled when she was able to reunite husbands with their wives and fathers with their children. But, too often, she had the unhappy task of telling a family that the soldier it loved was dead.

Soon Barton's organization was known throughout the United States. One man who had heard of it traveled hundreds of miles to see Barton. Introducing himself as Dorence Atwater, he explained that during the war he had been a prisoner at Andersonville, a Southern jail in Georgia. Because of his good penmanship, he was ordered by prison guards to keep a list of the Northern soldiers who had died and were buried there. Atwater gave the list to the guards. But all the time, he had a secret plan. Knowing that the Southerners would not bother to contact the families of the Northern dead, Atwater kept a copy of the list hidden in the lining of his coat. When he handed it to Barton, she was stunned. It included 13,000 names.

Using Atwater's list and her own correspondence, Barton was able to locate more than 22,000 missing men in 4 years. The work took a great deal of time. It also took a great deal of money, which she paid out of her own pocket. Congress promised to pay her back, but it was slow in giving her the funds. In the meantime, she was desperately in need of money.

Barton knew from experience that it could take a long time for a woman to find a job, too long considering that she had no savings left. But there was a simple solution to her financial problems. She knew people were fascinated by her war

Barton's exciting speeches about her experiences as a Civil War nurse always drew large audiences.

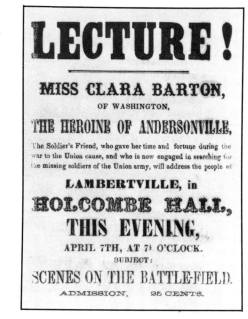

LECTURE!

MISS CLARA BARTON,
OF WASHINGTON,

THE HEROINE OF ANDERSONVILLE,

The Soldier's Friend, who gave her time and fortune during the war to the Union cause, and who is now engaged in searching for the missing soldiers of the Union army, will address the people of

LAMBERTVILLE, in

HOLCOMBE HALL,

THIS EVENING,

APRIL 7TH, AT 7½ O'CLOCK.

SUBJECT:

SCENES ON THE BATTLE-FIELD.

ADMISSION,   25 CENTS.

stories, fascinated enough to pay to hear them. Barton set out on a lecture tour with other famous speakers, including popular writers Mark Twain and Ralph Waldo Emerson.

Barton was a good speaker. Everywhere she went, she found a large, eager audience. But the work did not suit her well. "All speech-making terrifies me," she said. "First I have no taste for it, lastly I hate it."

One night in Boston, her fear and exhaustion got the better of her. Standing at a podium, she laid her notes in front of her, preparing to give a lecture to a packed room. Barton looked up and saw hundreds of pairs of eyes on her. The room was silent. She opened her mouth to speak, but still no noise could be heard. Like years earlier in Bordentown, she had lost her voice. Humiliated, Barton collected her notes and stumbled off the stage.

Her doctors told her she needed a long rest. After all, she had barely had a moment of quiet since the beginning of the war. Barton agreed and in 1869 boarded a ship bound for Europe.

She traveled through England and France and gradually recovered her strength. Feeling much better, she decided to visit Switzerland to see the beautiful city of Geneva. Barton had no idea at the time that this would be one of the most important decisions of her life.

While Barton was in Geneva, a physician named Louis Appia came to visit her. She had never heard of him, but Appia knew all about her. Barton's reputation was now so great that she was famous even in Europe.

Appia told her that her courage on the battlefield reminded him of the experiences of another wartime nurse—Jean-Henri Dunant. A wealthy Swiss banker, Dunant in 1859 had volunteered to give food and water to soldiers wounded in the Battle of Solferino, which pitted French forces against Austrian troops. Like Barton, Dunant was haunted by the soldiers he saw suffer needlessly because they did not get immediate medical care. His book *A Memory of Solferino* described the horrors he had seen. It also offered a solution. Dunant proposed that teams of volunteers be trained in peacetime. Then, in time of war, there would be no shortage of medical help. Wounded soldiers of all nations would receive care.

Dunant's dream became real in 1863. Representatives of 16 nations met in Geneva and agreed to form societies of volunteer medical personnel. The next year, the nations made the agreement official by signing the Treaty of Geneva.

At the signing, a very important question was asked: How could the volunteers be protected from attack on the battlefield? Everyone agreed that the volunteers should wear armbands bearing some type of special symbol so that soldiers would know not to shoot at them. As a tribute to Switzerland for hosting the meeting, the representatives decided that the symbol would look like the Swiss flag but with the colors reversed. So, the flag's white cross on a red background became a red cross on a white background. Along with the new symbol, the volunteer societies got a new name. From then on, they were known as the Red Cross.

Barton listened hard when Appia told her about the Red Cross. She was surprised she had never heard of it before. But Appia was not. As he explained to Barton, the United States was the only major nation in the world that had not agreed to sign the Treaty of Geneva.

Barton had no idea why this was so. Why would the United States not want to be involved with such a worthwhile organization as the Red Cross? She vowed to find out, but before she could return to the United States she would discover firsthand just how important the work of the Red Cross was.

On July 19, 1870, France declared war on Prussia, which later became part of Germany. For the first time, Red Cross volunteers were called into action. Even though Barton was still recovering from her illness, she felt she had to do what she could to help them.

She first traveled to Basel, Switzerland, where she worked making bandages. Barton was impressed by the Red Cross's well-stocked warehouses and well-trained workers. But the work made her restless. As she sat rolling cloth, the sky above was red with cannon fire. Barton could not help feeling she would be of more use at the front.

With a young Swiss woman named Antoinette Margot, Barton set out for the front lines.

The French city of Strasbourg witnessed one of the bloodiest battles in the Franco-Prussian War.

Along the way, they met hundreds of French families that had fled from their homes to escape the fighting. The French all begged the nurses to turn back before they were killed by German troops. But, already knowing the danger, Barton and Margot pressed on.

Riding on a horse-drawn bus, they headed for the city of Haguenau, where they had heard the fighting was heaviest. Suddenly, German soldiers approached them and ordered them to halt. An American flag was attached to the front of the bus to show troops that the riders were neutral, siding neither with France nor with Prussia. But the Germans did not recognize the flag. Suspicious of Barton and Margot, the soldiers refused to let them pass. Then Barton got an idea. She took off a red ribbon she was wearing around her neck and pulled a sewing kit out of her bag. In a minute, she had stitched a red-ribbon cross onto the sleeve of her dress. This was a symbol the guards understood. With a smile and a bow, one soldier waved the bus on. Barton proudly had just be-

As a Red Cross volunteer, Barton was able to persuade German soldiers to allow her to go to the front.

come the first American ever to wear the sign of the Red Cross on her arm.

After the war had ended with a victory for Germany, Barton kept working in Europe for the Red Cross. But by late 1873, the hard work had taken its toll. Ill and exhausted once again, she decided to return to the United States.

The next few years were not happy ones. Barton spent much of her time in bed. Often she was so weak she could not get up. Barton eventually went to a hospital in Danville, New York, for an extended stay. There, with good food and plenty of rest, her condition improved.

Even during this hard time, Barton never forgot the Red Cross. She wrote to Appia frequently, and he sent her letters describing the organization's progress. Gustave Moynier, president of the International Red Cross, also corresponded with Barton. He sent her a letter for the president of the United States, Rutherford B. Hayes, and asked her to deliver it personally. The letter was a request that the United States create its own branch of the Red Cross. It also named Barton as the organization's official American representative. Charged with such an important mission, Barton found the strength to rise from her sickbed. Like so many times before, she forgot about everything except the work she had to do.

Before retiring at age 83, Barton served as president of the American Red Cross for 23 years.

5

The American Red Cross in Action

On January 3, 1878, Barton sat in the White House, waiting to meet with the president of the United States. She could not help but be nervous. The entire future of the American Red Cross depended on the conversation she was about to have.

To her relief, President Hayes and his wife, Lucy, greeted her cordially. She gave the president Moynier's letter and told him all about the Red Cross. Hayes seemed very interested in what Barton had to say but told her she needed to speak with another important official, the attorney general, before anything could be done.

Barton met with the attorney general, who sent her to see the secretary of state, who in turn sent her to his assistant, Frederick W. Seward. Finally, Barton found in Seward someone willing to give her a straight answer, but it was not the answer she had hoped to hear. Unlike the other officials, Seward did know something about the Red Cross. He made it clear, though, that he did not care to know more. He told Barton the United States would never join the organization. Years ago, U.S. officials had considered signing the Treaty of Geneva but decided not to. They were afraid that if they did, European countries would think that they had the right to meddle in all sorts of affairs of the U.S. government. When Barton told him this would not happen, Seward gave another reason. Why should we sign the treaty, he said, if the United States was not planning to go to war?

Barton left Seward's office disappointed but not defeated. She realized that words could not convince the government to establish a Red Cross branch but action might. Maybe if the president could see for himself what the Red Cross could do, he would help Barton.

In 1881, Barton and some friends founded the American National Red Cross Society. The members elected Barton president. Although the society was not yet formally part of the International Red Cross, it was modeled after the official Red Cross branches in Europe. The one difference was that Barton wanted her organization to help not only wounded soldiers but also victims of natural disasters such as earthquakes and floods.

The society's creation was well timed. Only months later, a tremendous forest fire broke out in northern Michigan. The society sent volunteers and more than $80,000 worth of supplies to the disaster site.

In the spring of 1882, Barton was again in Washington, D.C. This time, she did not have to ask to see the president. President Chester A. Arthur, who had just taken office, had requested a meeting with her. Barton's plan had worked. Having learned about her organization's relief efforts in Michigan, Arthur told Barton that he was ready to sign the Treaty of Geneva. When he did, the American Red Cross would become an official branch of the International Red Cross. Barton then did something before the president that she seldom did in public: She wept.

In her first years as president of the American Red Cross, Barton was kept very busy. Almost every year there was a disaster somewhere in the United States, and the Red Cross was called in to help. Volunteers rushed to Ohio and Indiana to aid flood victims, to Louisiana and Alabama to help survivors of a tornado, and to South Carolina to provide relief after an earthquake.

The worst disaster of all happened in Johnstown, Pennsylvania. The city lay between a creek and a river. The inhabitants had learned to expect small floods to follow spring rains. But in the spring of 1889, the rains were heavier than normal. The floodwater in some parts of Johns-town rose to 13 feet. So much water collected in a nearby dam that its walls burst. A 30-foot-high wave rushed into the city, leveling all the buildings in its path. Thousands of people were killed as the water poured through the streets.

With this 1881 poster, the Red Cross asked for contributions of money, clothing, and bedding for victims of forest fires in Michigan.

MICHIGAN'S

TERRIBLE CALAMITY.

DANSVILLE SOCIETY OF THE

✚

RED CROSS.

A CRY FOR HELP!

The Dansville Society of the Red Cross, whose duty it is to accumulate funds and material, to provide nurses and assistants if may be, and hold these for use or service in case of war, or other national calamity—has heard the cry for help from Michigan. Senator O. D. Conger wrote on the 9th of September that he had just returned from the burnt region. Bodies of more than 200 persons had already been buried, and more than 1500 families had been burned out of everything. That was in only twenty townships in two counties. He invoked the aid of all our people. The character and extent of the calamity cannot be described in words. The manifold horrors of the fire were multiplied by fearful tornadoes, which cut off retreat in every direction. In some places whole families have been found reduced to an undistinguishable heap of wasted and blackened blocks of flesh, where they fell together overwhelmed by the rushing flames. For the dead, alas! there is nothing but burial. For the thousands who survive, without shelter, without clothing, without food, whose every vestige of a once happy home has been swept away, haply much, everything, can be done. The Society of the Red Cross of Dansville proposes to exercise its functions in this emergency, and to see to it that sympathy, money, clothing, bedding, everything wh'c'h those entirely destitute can need, shall find its way promptly to them. But the society is in its infancy here. It has in fact barely completed its organization. It has not in possession for immediate use the funds and stores which will in future be accumulated for such emergencies. It calls therefore upon the generous people of Dansville and vicinity to make at once such contributions, money or clothing, as their liberal hearts and the terrible exigency must prompt them to make. Our citizens will be called upon for cash subscriptions, or such subscriptions may be left with James Faulkner, Jr., Treasurer of the Society, at the First National Bank of Dansville. Contributions of Clothing and Bedding may be left at 154 Main street, Maxwell Block, Sewing Machine Agency of Mrs. John Sheppard.

☞ A special agent of the Society will be dispatched with the money and goods to see to their proper distribution. Please act promptly.

EXECUTIVE COMMITTEE RED CROSS.

Dansville, Sept. 13, 1881.

DANSVILLE ADVERTISER STEAM PRINT.

Barton arrived five days later on the first train that could get through. From a tent that served as Red Cross headquarters, she organized volunteers to feed the survivors and build temporary shelters for them. For five months, the Red Cross labored to clean up the wreckage. When its work was done, an editorial in the local newspaper said, "We cannot thank Miss Barton in words. Hunt the dictionaries of all languages through and you will not find the signs to express our appreciation for her and her work."

Although Barton spent much of her time at disaster areas, her great energy allowed her to pursue other interests. One was campaigning for women's rights. In Barton's day, women could not vote. This struck her as ridiculous. As a woman, she was regarded by the laws of the United States as too unintelligent and uninformed to vote for the very senators and presidents she had advised over the years. Many people agreed with Barton that the policy made no sense. They organized conventions to discuss ways to convince the government to give all women the vote. Throughout the East, Barton spoke at many such conventions, using stories of her and other women's accomplishments as evidence that women are the equals of men.

Barton also found time to travel to Europe as a U.S. representative to several annual conferences of the International Red Cross. The 1884 conference was especially memorable. The leaders of the International Red Cross decided that Barton's idea of providing disaster relief was a good one. All agreed to amend the Treaty of Geneva so that Red Cross chapters throughout the world could distribute supplies and dispatch volunteers in times of peace as well as in times of war. The conference representatives cheered Barton as speaker after speaker praised her enormous contributions to the Red Cross.

Other trips Barton made overseas were not as gratifying. In 1893, she went to Turkey, a country in Asia where a brutal religious war was raging. The American Red Cross brought relief to thousands of towns and villages that had no other hope of receiving aid. Five years later, Barton traveled to battlefields closer to home. The people of Cuba, an island about 100 miles south of Florida, were rising up against the Spaniards who ruled them. U.S. forces joined the Cubans in their fight.

The conflict, known as the Spanish-American War, was one of the bloodiest Barton had

Barton and other Red Cross volunteers helped rebuild Johnstown, Pennsylvania. The town was almost destroyed by a flood in 1889.

ever seen. To her disgust, the U.S. Army was again ill prepared to treat all the casualties. "It is the Civil War all over," Barton declared angrily. "No improvement in a third of a century."

Among the wounded the American Red Cross helped in the Spanish-American War were the Rough Riders, a volunteer regiment headed by Colonel Theodore Roosevelt. Roosevelt arrived at the Red Cross headquarters in Cuba desperate for supplies for his men. He asked the personnel there how much the supplies would cost. A Red Cross doctor replied that their supplies were not for sale, "not for a million dollars." The colonel's face fell. He wondered out loud how he could possibly get the food and medicine he needed. The doctor then smiled and said, "Just ask for them, Colonel." Roosevelt politely did and was soon heading back into the jungle, carrying a huge sack of supplies to his regiment.

When Barton returned to the United States, she was convinced that the Red Cross's efforts in Cuba had been a triumphant success. She believed their volunteers and supplies had made up for the army's poor planning and helped the United States and Cuba win the war. But some Red Cross workers believed otherwise. The influential New York chapter criticized Barton, saying that the work of the Red Cross in Cuba would have been much more effective if the relief efforts had been better organized. The New York chapter's leader, Mabel Boardman, said that Barton ought to resign the Red Cross presidency. According to Boardman, if the American Red Cross was to grow, it needed new leadership with new ideas. Barton, now in her eighties, was just too old to do the job.

Boardman's complaints were not completely unfounded. Barton's Red Cross was a small organization, largely because Barton preferred going to battlefields and disaster sites to staying in Washington and seeking more volunteers and contributions. Barton also was not good at giving others responsibility. Over many years, she had changed from a shy young girl to a confident elderly woman. She had finally learned to trust herself, but she had not learned to trust many other people. With Barton in charge, the American Red Cross would never become much larger than the small circle of Barton's friends and followers.

Barton was deeply hurt by Boardman's criticism. But she was devastated in 1902, when the U.S. government accused her of spending Red Cross funds on herself. The charges were unfair— Barton had actually spent much of her own money on the Red Cross. She could barely believe that the United States, which she had loved and served for so many years, would try to tarnish her reputation. Especially hurtful was that the accusations came from Theodore Roosevelt. The colonel who had begged for the Red Cross's help in Cuba was now the president of the United States. Instead of being grateful for what the Red Cross had done for him years before, he was attacking the heart of the organization.

After an investigation, all charges against Barton were dropped. But Barton was exhausted by the entire affair. She resigned as president of the Red Cross in 1904.

In retirement, Barton remained interested in the activities of the Red Cross, but after decades of work she was ready for a long rest. During her last years, she read many books on astrology and faith healing, subjects that had always interested her but that she had never before had the chance to study. Another favorite activity was tending the garden at her home in Glen Echo, Maryland.

Pansy carved from amethyst

Smoky topaz with pearls

Iron Cross of Imperial Germany

Cross of Imperial Russia

International Red Cross medal

Masonic emblem

Many foreign leaders honored Barton with medals and gifts of jewelry. She wore them with pride during the last years of her life.

Barton's friends remembered that while weeding and planting she often liked to wear the medals she had been awarded from foreign governments for her service. She had received so many that they covered the front of her dress.

At the age of 90, Clara Barton died of double pneumonia on April 13, 1912. She is now largely remembered as the founder of the American Red Cross, which today has almost 3,000 chapters and 20,000 employees. But, in a time when women were seldom permitted to be anything but wives and mothers, she excelled in several careers. She was a teacher who introduced new ideas about education to many communities. She was a nurse who helped ease the suffering of hundreds of people during one of the United States's bloodiest wars. And she was a diplomat who influenced the most powerful politicians both in Washington and in foreign lands. A woman who once claimed to have been afraid of "everything," Barton had a long life marked with feats of courage and strength.

Chronology

Dec. 25, 1821	Clara Barton born in North Oxford, Massachusetts
1832–34	Nurses her brother, David
1839	Earns her teaching certificate and begins teaching
1850	Enrolls at the Clinton Liberal Institute
1852	Begins teaching in Bordentown, New Jersey, and establishes a free public school
1854	Hired as a clerk in the U.S. Patent Office in Washington, D.C.

1857	Loses job and returns to North Oxford
1860	Takes temporary job with the Patent Office
April 14, 1861	The Civil War begins; Barton nurses Union soldiers
1862	Surgeon general issues Barton a military pass that allows her to nurse the wounded at the battlefront
1863	Red Cross founded in Geneva, Switzerland
April 9, 1865	Civil War ends
1865	Barton begins a nationwide search for missing soldiers
1869	Sails to Europe; meets with representatives of the Red Cross
1870–71	Works with the Red Cross during the Franco-Prussian War
1873	Returns to the United States
1881	Establishes the American Red Cross Society
March 16, 1882	Congress ratifies the Treaty of Geneva, enabling the United States to join the International Committee of the Red Cross

1884	Leaders of the International Red Cross amend the Treaty of Geneva to allow disaster relief
1889	Barton organizes relief efforts after the Johnstown flood
1898	Helps victims of the Spanish-American War
1902	U.S. government accuses Barton of spending Red Cross funds on herself
1904	Barton resigns as president of the Red Cross
April 13, 1912	Clara Barton dies of double pneumonia

Glossary

abolitionist   in U.S. history, particularly in the decades before the Civil War, a member of the movement to end slavery

attorney general   the chief law officer of the United States

bloodletting   a treatment in which leeches are placed on a patient's body in the belief that they will suck out disease-causing blood

boarding school   a school at which meals and housing are provided

Congress   the lawmaking body of the United States

diplomat   a person who conducts negotiations between nations

International Red Cross   founded in 1863; a volunteer organization that provides aid during wars or natural disasters

leeches bloodsucking worms

musket a shoulder gun used by foot soldiers

phrenology the study that holds that people's characters and special talents are caused by the shape of the brain and skull

Rough Riders during the Spanish-American War, a volunteer regiment headed by future president Theodore Roosevelt

secretary of state the chief foreign policy administrator for the United States

smallpox a contagious disease that causes high fever and severe skin rashes

surgeon general the chief medical officer of the United States

Treaty of Geneva an agreement signed by 16 nations in 1864 and by the United States in 1882 that established the International Red Cross

U.S. Patent Office the government agency that guarantees to the inventor of a new product or process the sole rights to the production, use, and sale of his or her work

women's rights movement the movement to obtain for women all of the rights that men have

Picture Credits

American Red Cross: pp. 2, 32, 46; The Bettmann Archive: pp. 6, 23, 56, 58, 60; Clara Barton National Historic Site, Glen Echo, MD: pp. 10, 16, 18, 72; Historical Society of Pennsylvania: p. 68; Library of Congress: pp. 13, 28, 38, 41, 44, 51; Michigan Department of State: p. 65

Liz Sonneborn is an editor living in New York City.